CW00523956

Glenda Jackson

Biography of Glenda Jackson, Cause of
death, net worth, age, relationship,
career, family and more.

by

Justin Riley

Table of Contents

Chapter 1

Biography of Glenda Jackson

Glenda Jackson, a remarkable figure in modern British history, has overcome humble beginnings to achieve incredible success. Known for her intelligence and meticulous work ethic, she has made a name for herself as both an acclaimed actress and a respected Member of Parliament (MP). Born into a working-class family in Birkenhead, with a bricklayer father and a mother who worked as a cleaning lady, Jackson experienced a life-changing event when her father joined the Navy and served on a minesweeper. Despite the modest circumstances, she showed great promise from an early age.

Completing her education at the age of 16, Jackson initially found work at a pharmacy.

However, she quickly realized that this path offered limited prospects and sought a more fulfilling career. At the age of 18, her life took a transformative turn when she was accepted into the prestigious Royal Academy of Dramatic Art (RADA). Her talent and dedication impressed everyone who witnessed her performances. Around this time, she also married Roy Hodges, marking another significant milestone in her personal life.

Jackson's first notable work was on the stage, where she garnered praise from both critics and audiences alike for her role in the adaptation of "Separate Tables." This success opened doors for her in the film industry, although initially in supporting roles. With unwavering determination, she approached each opportunity with great enthusiasm. Her breakthrough moment came when she secured a supporting role in the controversial film "Marat/Sade" in 1967, where she is widely acknowledged to have stolen the show. This marked her entrance into Britain's A-List, and her career soared from there.

In 1968, Jackson received her first leading role in the offbeat drama "Negatives," shining brightly even in unconventional material. The following year, renowned director Ken Russell cast her as the lead in his adaptation of the 1920s romance "Women in Love," alongside Oliver Reed. The beautifully crafted film became a major success, and Jackson's outstanding performance earned her an Academy Award for Best Actress, propelling her to international stardom. Despite the newfound fame and recognition, she remained grounded and placed greater value on her craft than on the status it brought. This commitment led her to collaborate with Russell on more films, including the controversial "The Music Lovers" (1971), where she had to confront her discomfort with a nude scene. Although the film did not achieve commercial success, Jackson's cameo appearance in Russell's next film, "The Boy Friend" (1971), once again showcased her exceptional talent.

The year 1971 proved pivotal for Jackson's career. She took on a risk by starring in "Sunday Bloody Sunday" as a divorced businesswoman involved in a dead-end affair with a shallow bisexual artist. The film turned out to be another major success, solidifying her reputation as a versatile and captivating performer. Additionally, she portrayed Queen Elizabeth I in the highly anticipated biographical television series "Elizabeth R" for the British Broadcasting Corporation (BBC). Her portrayal was not only praised by critics and fans but also recognized by historians as the most accurate representation of the beloved former queen. That same year, she reprised the role of Queen Elizabeth I in the historical drama "Mary, Queen of Scots." Furthermore, Jackson displayed her comedic talent in a memorable skit as Queen Cleopatra on the popular comedy series "The Morecambe & Wise Show" (1968). This showcased her ability to excel in both comedic and dramatic roles. Director Melvin Frank, who witnessed her comedic brilliance, subsequently cast her in the romantic comedy "A Touch of Class" (1973), where her chemistry with co-star George Segal elevated the film to a major hit and earned her a second Academy Award.

Throughout her career, Jackson remained committed to seeking out challenging and artistically stimulating roles, prioritizing substance over commercial success. She delivered strong performances in films like "The Romantic Englishwoman" (1975) and "The Incredible Sarah" (1976), where she portrayed the legendary actress Sarah Bernhardt. However, some of her films, such as "The Triple Echo" (1972), "The Maids" (1975), and "Nasty Habits" (1977), did not resonate with the public as expected.

Moreover, amidst her professional endeavors, her marriage fell apart in 1976. Despite these personal and professional challenges, Jackson's career continued to flourish, and in 1978 she was honored with the title of Commander of the Order of the British Empire.

In 1978, Jackson made a successful comeback with the comedy film "House Calls," starring alongside Walter Matthau. The film's success paved the way for a popular television spin-off in the United States the following year. In 1979, she reunited with George Segal in "Lost and Found," although the film failed to overcome its predictable script. Another collaboration with Oliver Reed in "The Class of Miss MacMichael" (1978) also yielded disappointing results. Despite these setbacks, Jackson's talent and dedication remained unwavering.

As the 1980s unfolded, Jackson continued to act while increasingly focusing on public affairs. Having grown up in a household that staunchly supported the Labour Party, she held strong political opinions. Jackson openly expressed her disapproval of Conservative Prime Minister Margaret Thatcher's policies, even though she acknowledged some of Thatcher's personal attributes. Furthermore, she strongly disagreed with Thatcher's successor, John Major. Discontent with the direction of British government policies, Jackson decided to run for Parliament in 1992. Although her party faced challenges in the Hampstead and Highgate area, she won by a narrow margin and quickly became one of the most prominent newly elected members.

Contrary to expectations, Jackson did not rest on her laurels and celebrity status but instead actively engaged in various political issues. In 1997, she was appointed Junior Transportation Minister by Prime Minister

Tony Blair, focusing her efforts on transportation-related matters. However, despite her role within the government, she remained critical of some of Blair's policies, establishing herself as an inter-party opponent of Blair's moderate faction. As a traditional Labour Party activist, she distanced herself from the faction known as The Looney Left.

In 2000, Jackson sought the Labour Party nomination for the Mayor of London but lost to fellow MP Frank Dobson, an ally of Blair's. However, Dobson himself lost the election to independent candidate Ken Livingstone. Undeterred, Jackson made another attempt in 2005 and secured the nomination but ultimately lost to Livingstone, garnering 38% of the vote. Speculation about Jackson's potential as a successor to Blair as Prime Minister emerged when he announced he would not seek re-election in 2006. However, Jackson did not actively encourage such speculation.

In 2010, Jackson faced a close race for re-election to Parliament, narrowly winning by a margin of only 42 votes. Her resilience and commitment to public service were evident throughout her career. In 2013, upon the death of Margaret Thatcher, she publicly expressed her strong opposition to Thatcher's policies, a stance that received mixed reactions and was deemed by some as lacking grace. When parliamentary elections were held again in 2015, Jackson opted not to seek re-election, and she was succeeded in Parliament by Chris Philip, a Conservative Party member who had previously been her opponent in 2010.

Glenda Jackson's journey from humble beginnings to becoming an accomplished actress and respected Member of Parliament is a testament to her unwavering determination, intelligence, and passion for her craft. Her remarkable career has spanned decades, marked by outstanding performances, critical acclaim, and prestigious awards. Despite facing personal and professional challenges along the way, Jackson's commitment to artistic integrity and her unwavering political beliefs have remained constant.

Beyond her accomplishments in the entertainment industry and politics, Glenda Jackson has made a lasting impact on British society through her activism and advocacy. Throughout her career, she has been a vocal champion for causes close to her heart, using her platform to shed light on social issues and fight for justice. Her involvement in transportation issues early in her parliamentary career demonstrated her dedication to improving the lives of everyday citizens.

Jackson's alignment with the Labour Party and her staunch opposition to conservative policies have positioned her as a formidable force within the political landscape. Her unwavering commitment to her principles, even in the face of opposition, has earned her respect and admiration from supporters and fellow activists alike.

While her political career has had its ups and downs, Jackson's influence extends beyond her time in office. Her legacy as a trailblazer and an advocate for social justice continues to inspire younger generations. Her dedication to public service and her unyielding pursuit of truth and fairness serve as a reminder of the power of individuals to effect meaningful change.

As Glenda Jackson's career transitions into new chapters, it is clear that her impact will extend far beyond the stage and the halls of Parliament. Her legacy as a multi-talented artist, a principled politician, and a passionate advocate will forever be etched in the annals of British history. Few individuals have risen from humble beginnings to achieve such heights, and

Glenda Jackson's remarkable journey serves as a testament to the indomitable human spirit and the pursuit of excellence against all odds.

Chapter 2

Career

Jackson's involvement in Lindsay Anderson's film "This Sporting Life" marked her initial foray into the world of cinema, albeit in a brief role. However, it was two years later, when she portrayed the boldly sensual character Gudrun in Ken Russell's adaptation of D.H. Lawrence's novel "Women in Love," that her acting career truly soared. This performance proved to be a turning point as she garnered recognition and acclaim, ultimately earning two prestigious Academy Awards for Best Actress. Remarkably, she declined to attend the award ceremonies to accept these honors.

Throughout her career, Jackson remained vocal about the dearth of positive and substantial roles available for women.

Despite this, she managed to find such roles well into her fifties. Then, in a stunning turn of events, she made a courageous decision that shockcd the industry: she relinquished her fame and embarked on a new path in politics. In 1992, she won an election and became a Member of Parliament representing the London neighborhoods of Hampstead and Kilburn, effectively leaving behind her prior achievements in the world of entertainment. This dedication to public service endured until 2015 when she resigned from her political position.

Following a triumphant return to the stage, where she portrayed the iconic character King Lear, Jackson continued to receive accolades for her work. Notably, she received another prestigious award for her compelling performances as two distinct characters: the stumbling and acerbic 92-year-old widow in a Broadway revival of Edward Albee's "Three Tall Women," and Maud, the protagonist suffering from

Alzheimer's disease in "Elizabeth Is Missing."

In her later years, Jackson decided to abandon her residence in north London and instead opted for a more modest basement apartment located in her son Dan Hodges' home in south London. It is worth mentioning that Dan Hodges, at the time, was a political columnist and held views that diverged significantly from his mother's. Within the confines of this cozy abode, she dedicated herself to gardening, witnessed the growth of her beloved grandson, and maintained her sharp wit, never shying away from criticizing any form of foolishness or hypocrisy that crossed her path.

Chapter 3

Family and Relationship

In a union that spanned nearly two decades, Glenda Jackson, the renowned British actress and politician, entered into the sacred institution of marriage with Roy Hodges in 1958. Their journey as life partners continued until 1976, encompassing a significant chapter of their lives together.

Glenda Jackson, a remarkable individual known for her exceptional talent and unwavering dedication to her craft, achieved great acclaim in both the realms of acting and politics. Throughout their marriage, Glenda and Roy shared numerous experiences, creating a bond that weathered the tests of time. Together, they navigated the ups and downs, the joys and challenges that life invariably presents.

Sadly, the journey of Glenda Jackson and Roy Hodges as a married couple eventually came to an end, and they decided to part ways in 1976. While the details surrounding their separation are not widely known, it marked a significant transition in their lives and led them on separate paths.

Although their marital journey concluded, Glenda Jackson's life continued to unfold, and she embarked on a remarkable journey as a mother. Glenda and Roy were blessed with a child, whom they named Daniel Pearce Jackson Hodges. Daniel, a testament to their enduring love, became the embodiment of their shared experiences and a cherished legacy of their time together.

As Glenda Jackson continued to make an indelible mark on the world through her remarkable acting career and later in her political endeavors, she carried with her the memories of her marriage to Roy Hodges. While their union had its conclusion, the impact of their time together resonated throughout Glenda's life, shaping her perspectives and influencing her path.

Today, Glenda Jackson's legacy lives on, not only through her groundbreaking achievements but also through the love and connection she shared with her son Daniel. As she left an indelible mark on the world through her talent and accomplishments, Glenda's role as a mother to Daniel remained a source of profound joy and fulfillment.

In reflecting upon the life of Glenda Jackson, we celebrate her remarkable journey as an actress, a politician, and a mother. We acknowledge the role that Roy Hodges played in her life, as a partner during their marriage and as the father of their beloved child, Daniel. Through the ebb and flow of their relationship, Glenda's resilience and determination shone through, inspiring those around her and leaving an enduring legacy for generations to come.

Chapter 4

Age

Jackson, a remarkable individual whose life began in the year 1936, graced the world with her presence in the picturesque town of Birkenhead, located in the enchanting county of Merseyside. As fate would have it, she emerged as the first-born daughter among her loving parents' brood of four daughters. Her father, a diligent bricklayer, poured his sweat and toil into constructing sturdy foundations, while her mother embraced the noble task of cleaning, ensuring the sanctity of their humble abode.

Throughout the passage of time, Jackson embarked on a journey enriched with experiences, challenges, and moments that shaped her into the exceptional individual she would become. The world witnessed the unfolding of history as she traversed through the tumultuous chapters of the 20th and early 21st centuries, witnessing significant social, cultural, and technological transformations that left an indelible mark on the fabric of society.

A testament to her strength and resilience, Jackson defied the odds and gracefully embraced the golden age of her life, a remarkable 87-year journey marked by countless milestones and cherished memories. Her days were a tapestry woven with the threads of joy, sorrow, triumphs, and setbacks, all contributing to the rich mosaic of her existence.

As the hands of time continued their eternal dance, the hourglass emptied, and Jackson bid farewell to the mortal realm, her legacy echoing through the corridors of time. The profound impact she made on the lives of those around her, her unwavering determination, and the wisdom she imparted will forever resonate in the hearts and minds of those fortunate enough to have crossed paths with her.

Though she may no longer be physically present, her spirit endures, and the memories of her remarkable life continue to inspire and guide future generations. Her tale serves as a reminder of the inherent strength that lies within the human spirit, a beacon of hope in the face of adversity, and a testament to the power of love, family, and resilience.

In celebrating the life of Jackson, we pay homage to the countless lessons she imparted, the unwavering love she shared, and the profound impact she made on the world. May her soul find eternal peace, and may her memory be forever etched in the annals of history, serving as a constant reminder of the extraordinary legacy she left behind.

Chapter 5

Net Worth

Before her passing, Glenda Jackson had amassed an approximate net worth of $5 million, a testament to her successful career and financial achievements. The late Glenda Jackson, renowned for her exceptional talent and remarkable contributions to the world of entertainment, had secured a significant fortune through her various professional endeavors.

Glenda Jackson, a prominent figure in the realm of acting, captivated audiences across the globe with her unparalleled performances and magnetic on-screen presence. Her multifaceted career spanned decades and encompassed a wide range of roles in both film and theater, earning her critical acclaim, numerous accolades, and a dedicated fan base.

Throughout her illustrious journey, Glenda Jackson meticulously crafted her craft, effortlessly embodying a plethora of diverse characters that resonated deeply with viewers. Whether it was a complex and enigmatic protagonist or a supporting role that left an indelible mark, her undeniable talent and dedication to her craft set her apart from her peers.

Beyond her artistic endeavors, Glenda Jackson demonstrated a keen business acumen, successfully leveraging her fame and influence to secure lucrative endorsement deals and brand partnerships. This entrepreneurial spirit, combined with her unwavering commitment to her craft, ultimately contributed to her impressive net worth.

Moreover, Glenda Jackson's financial success was not limited to her on-screen achievements alone. She ventured into various other avenues, including investments and real estate, ensuring a diversified portfolio that bolstered her financial stability and expanded her wealth. Through strategic decisions and prudent financial management, she navigated the complexities of the industry and solidified her position as a shrewd businesswoman.

While Glenda Jackson's passing marked a tremendous loss for the entertainment industry, her legacy lives on not only through her impactful body of work but also through the philanthropic efforts she championed during her lifetime. Recognizing the importance of giving back to society, she actively supported charitable causes close to her heart, using her platform and resources to make a positive difference in the lives of others.

In essence, Glenda Jackson's estimated net worth of $5 million before her demise stands as a testament to her extraordinary talent, unwavering dedication, and astute financial decisions. Through her unparalleled contributions to the world of entertainment, her entrepreneurial endeavors, and her philanthropic efforts, she left an indelible mark on both the industry she loved and the lives she touched, ensuring that her legacy endures for generations to come.

Chapter 6

Cause of Death

In a recent announcement, Glenda Jackson's representative, Lionel Larner, issued a heartfelt statement to commemorate the passing of this remarkable individual. The statement expressed the sad news that Glenda Jackson, a distinguished actress who had been bestowed with the prestigious Academy Award not once, but twice, in her illustrious career, had peacefully departed from this world. She breathed her last in the serene confines of her residence situated in the vibrant neighborhood of Blackheath in London. The solemn event took place during the early hours of the morning, enveloped by an atmosphere of calmness and tranquility.

Glenda Jackson's remarkable journey encompassed both the worlds of the silver screen and the realm of politics, rendering her a multifaceted personality who left an indelible mark on both domains. With a career spanning decades, she showcased her extraordinary acting prowess and mesmerized audiences around the globe with her captivating performances. Her immense talent and dedication to her craft earned her the distinction of being recognized by the esteemed Academy of Motion Picture Arts and Sciences not just once, but twice, attaining the pinnacle of success by receiving two Academy Awards.

However, Glenda Jackson's influence extended beyond the realm of acting, as she ventured into the sphere of politics, showcasing her unwavering commitment to public service. Her foray into politics exemplified her deep-rooted desire to effect positive change in society and use her platform to advocate for causes close to her heart. With a resolute spirit, she fearlessly embraced the challenges that come with the pursuit of political office, seeking to make a tangible difference and amplify the voices of those she represented.

Sadly, this exceptional journey has now come to an end. Glenda Jackson's final moments were surrounded by her beloved family, providing solace and support as she faced her brief illness with grace and dignity. As she took her last breath, the presence of loved ones in her cherished home brought comfort during this poignant chapter.

News of Glenda Jackson's passing reverberates throughout the entertainment industry, as colleagues and admirers alike mourn the loss of an exceptional talent and a true trailblazer. The impact of her contributions, both on and off the screen, will continue to resonate for generations to come, leaving an enduring legacy of inspiration and artistic brilliance.

In light of this somber news, the world pauses to reflect upon the extraordinary life of Glenda Jackson, remembering her as a consummate actress, a dedicated politician, and above all, a remarkable human being. Her memory will forever live on, etched in the annals of cinema and politics, as a testament to her enduring spirit and unwavering commitment to her craft and her ideals.

Printed in Great Britain
by Amazon

24376943R00020